Old Glasgow Streets

Rudolph Kenna

First published in 1990 by
Strathclyde Regional Archives
Mitchell Library
North Street
Glasgow G3 7DN

3rd Edition 1993

ISBN 0 9517010 0 2

A CIP catalogue record for this book is available from the British Library.

Typeset and printed by
Strathclyde Regional Council Printing Works,
197 Pollokshaws Road, Glasgow G41 1TL
Telephone 041-227 3836

Front Cover: Glasgow Bridge looking north, 1914.

Back Cover: Broomielaw west of Oswald Street, 1914.

Introduction

Britain's most successful post-industrial city was in previous centuries a cathedral town, an *entrepôt,* a cotton town, and the world's foremost centre of shipbuilding and heavy engineering. These successive incarnations left their mark on the street pattern of Glasgow.

Until the Reformation, the most important streets, occupied by the clergy and gentry, were in the medieval upper town. The first town centre of Glasgow, south-west of the Cathedral, was formed by the intersection of High Street, Rottenrow and Drygait. The craftsmen and traders lived in the lower town, contiguous to the River Clyde. Glasgow was a compact little city, contained within a number of gates or ports, including the Stable Green Port, the Gallowgate or East Port and the South Port or 'Nether Barras yett'. After the Reformation, the ecclesiastical town dwindled in importance. The new town centre was the present Glasgow Cross, situated where the four streets of the early merchant city converged. Glasgow's 'four fair streets', cruciform in plan, formed an intersection at the Mercat Cross. One arm of the cross was Trongait and Gallowgait, the other Saltmarket and High Street.

The streets of 17th century Glasgow, defiled by ashpits, dunghills and sewage water, were not for the squeamish. We can be tolerably certain that the Stinking Vennel lived up to its name. Until 1755, when a public slaughterhouse was erected, cattle were slaughtered in the streets. As late as 1795 haystacks stood on both sides of the Trongait.

Stringent regulations were applied to the town's lepers, accommodated in St. Ninian's Hospital on the south side of the Clyde, at Bridgend—another name for the ancient suburb of Gorbals. Inmates were only allowed into town on Wednesdays and Saturdays, between the hours of ten and two. They were to keep to the causeway side, avoiding the 'croon o' the causeway' used by the townsfolk, wear veils, and announce their approach by means of clappers. In time of plague, the town's ports were guarded by day and kept locked at night. Any burgess who failed to take his turn on guard duty, armed with a halberd, was subject to a fine of £5. Night life in 17th century Glasgow must have been conspicuous by its absence. In 1608 an act was passed prohibiting all persons from walking in the street after ten o'clock, on pain of a £10 fine.

The old merchant town in the vicinity of the Mercat Cross was largely built of wood and burned like tinder on the occasion of Glasgow's great fire in 1652. A second, less spectacular blaze in 1677 swept away most of the remaining timber houses. Afterwards the citizens prudently built in stone.

In 1723, that irrepressible 'true born Englishman' Daniel Defoe lavished praise on Glasgow, singling out the four principal streets of the town, 'The finest built that I have ever seen in one city together.' Nothing remains of the celebrated *piazzas* or arcaded streets, a much-admired feature of Glasgow Cross in the early 1700s. The tall narrow gabled facades, with their stone arcades at street level, must have resembled Gladstone's Land in Edinburgh's Lawnmarket. In 1736, according to Glasgow's first historian John McUre, the town consisted of ten principal streets and seventeen wynds or lanes.

Glasgow's first New Town, the Merchant City of today, was laid out in the late eighteenth century. Streets such as Miller Street and Virginia Street were formed on the strips of back garden ground (riggs) which ran north from Trongait. The second New Town, on Blythswood Hill, followed in the early 19th century. Fashionable Glasgow was set on its *Drang nach Westen,* spreading in successive waves of stone and mortar to Anniesland and, ultimately, to the 'Greater Glasgow' of Bearsden and Milngavie. The Old Town was abandoned to the poorest classes. In 1832 and 1848, cholera spread in the ill-ventilated, insanitary and grossly over-crowded wynds and closes off High Street, Saltmarket and Briggait. In 1866, when the first City Improvement Act was passed, the death rate in some of Glasgow's most congested districts was 30 per 1,000. In 1839 Lord Shaftesbury described the wynds in the central districts as 'small alleys, like gutters, crammed with houses, dunghills, and human beings.'

The Act of 1866, amended in 1880, set up a City Improvement Trust with powers of compulsory purchase. Between 1870 and 1876 5,075 houses were pulled down, displacing 25,375 tenants and lodgers. Seven 'model lodging houses' were built to provide shelter for some of these unfortunates. Under the two Improvement Acts of 1866 and 1897, the Trust had built only 2,199 houses by 1914. Far from being solved, the housing problem had merely been transferred to districts such as Cowcaddens, where large families inhabited 'single ends' (one roomed flats) and children played in sunless alleys and dismal backcourts.

Glasgow's approach to slum clearance has always been unsentimental, and the City Improvement Trust, with the best of intentions, committed some shocking acts of vandalism, with the result that the city has forfeited almost all vestiges of its more distant past. Provand's Lordship (1464) is all that remains of the medieval street architecture of Glasgow. There were once 31 similar houses in the vicinity of the Cathedral, prebendal manses of the clergy.

The desire to make a clean sweep again emerged in the aftermath of the Second World War. An incredible 29 Comprehensive Development Areas were proposed in 1957, only nine of which had been approved by 1980, a dispensation for which the people of Glasgow can be truly grateful. In the CDA years, 'slum' proved to be a very elastic term: whole districts were levelled in the indiscriminate manner more usually associated with the saturation bombing techniques of the Second World War. Gorbals was the first district to be redeveloped, and its notoriety ensured for it a 'final solution' of Draconian severity. High-rise dwellings, costly to build and maintain and anti-social in their effects, rose on the sites of Glasgow's tenement neighbourhoods.

Streets as we know them today are a comparatively recent innovation. In 1577 the magistrates of Glasgow had to bring a 'calsay maker' all the way from Dundee to undertake street causewaying in the town. There were no pavements until the late 18th century. In 1777, when 'handsome flagged trottoirs with curbstones' were laid down in Trongait and the Westergait (now Argyle Street), the Quality took to promenading with great regularity, secure in the knowledge that they were now able to do so without sinking into the mire.

At the beginning of the 18th century, street cleaning was extremely rudimentary, the night watchmen devoting two hours twice a week to the job. In 1767 one Alexander Brown secured the post of street cleaner at a salary of £48 sterling per annum. He had a lucrative perk, for he was allowed to keep the dung which he gathered from the streets—it was a valuable commodity in those days, so much so in fact, that householders formed 'fulzie' (manure) heaps in the streets outside their dwellings.

In the early 18th century, street lighting consisted of a few dim conical lamps fuelled by rapeseed and hempseed oil. The whole street lighting for the winter of 1738 cost only £47 4s 4½d sterling. In 1817 the Glasgow Gas Light Company was formed, and by the following year 1,472 gas lamps had been installed in the streets of the city. The Corporation took over the gas works in 1869. Glasgow's first superintendent of streets was appointed in 1818, and by the late 19th century, gas lighting, paving, sewers and regular scavenging had transformed the city's streets.

In 1848, the 'Year of Revolutions', Glasgow was the only city in Britain where street barricades were erected. They went up in the Saltmarket in March, but were soon removed by the military. Gunsmiths' premises were ransacked for muskets and other firearms, and there were cries of 'Bread or Revolution'. Sentencing one of the ringleaders to 18 years' transportation, Lord Medwyn advised the unemployed to trust to the benevolence of the rich and show gratitude for small mercies.

Despite a cavalier attitude towards ancient buildings, the Victorians made a huge contribution to the street architecture of Glasgow. Usually of four storeys, without basements or railed off areas, the tenements of Victorian Glasgow rose sheer and cliff-like, forming interminable stone canyons which were particularly imposing at night; '. . . great shadowy piles, impressive as a Roman amphitheatre,' was how James Hamilton Muir* described them in *Glasgow in 1901*. He compared Glasgow tenements, when lighted at night, to 'palaces en fête, with approaches as abrupt, and mean, and insignificant, as if the buildings rose from canals.'

Glasgow's New Towns of the 18th and 19th centuries were laid out on a rectangular plan, like the prairie cities of the United States. But there the resemblance ends. For the stately tenements and terraces of Glasgow marched over a large number of Ice Age drumlins. Names such as Garnethill, Partickhill and Dowanhill express the essential nature of the city's topography. Some Glasgow streets need only cable cars to complete the resemblance to San Francisco.

As late as 1750, Stockwellgait, where the Trongait ended, was Glasgow's western extremity. A century later, rural villages such as Anderston, Gorbals, Tradeston and Calton were incorporated within the city boundaries. As Glasgow expanded prodigiously, the need arose for some form of public transport other than sedan chairs, some of which were still plying for hire in the 1840s. Cabriolets—hackney carriages drawn by one horse—were first seen in Glasgow streets during the 1820s. In 1834 steam road carriages operated between Glasgow and Paisley, but in July of that year one of the vehicles exploded, killing four passengers, and the Court of Session intervened to prevent their further use.

In 1845 Robert Frame started an omnibus service from Bridgeton to Anderston at the low rate of 2d. By 1846 he had four buses on the road, but went bankrupt the following year. In the 1850s and 1860s the most successful operator was Andrew Menzies, who ran an efficient fleet of horse-drawn omnibuses, painted in distinctive Menzies tartan livery. At the peak of his activities, Menzies had 50 buses and 500 horses, stabled in a three-storey block in North Street. Glasgow's first tram, operated by the Glasgow Tramway and Omnibus Company, of which Menzies was managing director, ran in 1872 from St. George's Cross to Eglinton Toll.

The Corporation, in the best traditions of 'gas and water socialism', took the tramway service over in 1894 and reduced the minimum fare to a halfpenny. At the beginning of the twentieth century, cheap and reliable public transport linked the inner city with the new residential suburbs. Neil Munro's Jimmy Swan was thoroughly at home in Ibrox, served by the Subway and the electric tramcar. As late as the 1900s, Joseph Hansom's 'gondola of the streets' was a familiar sight in Glasgow, but it disappeared forever in the face of competition from the motorised taxi cab. In 1962 the trams followed the hansom cabs and the sedan chairs into oblivion, but there are plans afoot now to start a modern tram service on the south side of the city.

Some historic Glasgow streets have had several aliases, associated with changes in function. Saltmarket was originally Waulcergait, where the town's waulcers, or fullers plied their trade. Later the street came up in the world as a fine residential thoroughfare of stone mansions. Its present name recalls the salt used in the herring industry—according to Daniel Defoe, Glasgow's salt-cured herrings were the best in Britain. Trongait was at first known as St. Thenew's Gait, but the name was changed after the public weighbeam (or Tron) had been set up there.

Many old Glasgow street names disappeared in the successive rebuilding of the city, among them Balaam's Pass, Witch Loan and Lindsay's Wester Wynd, but a truncated portion of the famous Schipka Pass still survives, as does the pleasantly named Harmony Row in Govan. There is no longer a Stinking Vennel in Glasgow, but there is a Fifth Avenue and a Madison Avenue.

In some of Glasgow's oldest localities the wheel of change has turned full circle. Calton is again a district of small houses set in gardens. Strathclyde University has filled the vacuum left by Glasgow University in the 1870s, when it moved from the Old College to Gilmorehill. Rottenrow exemplifies the variegated fortunes of some of Glasgow's oldest streets. Before the Reformation, it housed ecclesiastical dignitaries and enjoyed high status. With the passing centuries, it lost caste, degenerating into a slum quarter, but has now acquired a new sense of purpose as part of Strathclyde University campus.

The old streets of Glasgow were enlivened by a host of eccentric characters such as Johnny Cockup, who walked with his head in the air, and the Ayrshire hermit, who never shaved or cut his hair after a youthful disappointment in love. What would Hawkie, Penny a Yard, Wee Jamie Wallace, Old Malabar, Rab Haw and the Clincher make of the multitude of performers who once again enliven the streets of a city undergoing its fifth transformation in eight hundred years?

*Composite pseudonym used by James Bone, Archibald Hamilton Charteris and Muirhead Bone.

Acknowledgements

The photographs are from Strathclyde Regional Archives with three exceptions. Acknowledgements are due to the Librarian of the Mitchell Library for permission to reproduce numbers 7, 8 and 12.

Tenements being erected at 85-105 Gorbals Street, Gorbals Cross, c.1870. In the foreground, doing duty as a rudimentary pub, are the remains of the chapel which once formed part of the 17th century mansion of Sir George Elphinstone of Blythswood. Under the City Improvement Act of 1866, old Gorbals Main Street was swept away, tenements of dressed stone replacing its rubble-built, often thatched, houses.

Bridge Street looking south from Carlton Place, c. 1870, with a cabriolet in the foreground and the pillared frontage of Bridge Street Station on the right.

Trongate in the 1870s looking west towards the Tolbooth and Tontine Hotel. The latter was destroyed by fire in 1911. One of Andrew Menzies' tartan buses can be seen in the foreground.

Charlotte Street, Calton, in the late 19th century. The Park Lane of Georgian Glasgow was laid out in 1779 and named in honour of the consort of George III. In 1783 David Dale, father of the Scottish cotton industry, built a handsome town residence at the Glasgow Green end of the street. His house later became an Eye Infirmary and a Salvation Army hostel. It was demolished in the 1950s for the extension of Our Lady and St. Francis School.

Buchanan Street looking south to St. Enoch's Square, c. 1885. The vista was closed by St. Enoch's Church, demolished in 1926. It was originally a residential street. Shops began to arrive in the 1820s as retailers moved west from the vicinity of Glasgow Cross, and by the turn of the century Buchanan Street had become Glasgow's most fashionable shopping centre and promenade.

Old Basin Tavern, Baird's Brae, Hamiltonhill, c. 1890. At the turn of the century, many long-established Glasgow hostelries were swept away and replaced by up-to-date premises—open-planned with island bars—conforming to the requirements of the crusading licensing authorities.

Hill Street looking west at the turn of the century, by which time Garnethill, perched high above Sauchiehall Street, was a cosmopolitan 'Little Montmartre' with a synagogue and a German Club.

Main Street, Anderston, in the late 19th century. The village was founded in 1725 by the Andersons of Stobcross. Comprehensive redevelopment obliterated the old street pattern of Anderston. The approximate site of Main Street is marked by the Anderston Cross Branch of the former Glasgow Savings Bank (1899-1900).

Langside Avenue looking west towards Pollokshaws Road, late 19th century. The ornamental drinking fountain was a product of Walter Macfarlane's Saracen Foundry. Similar fountains were exported to the British colonies and Dominions. The pub on the left, advertising Tennent's lager, occupies the site of the present Glasgow Style *Corona Bar* (1912).

Queen Street looking north from Exchange Square, c. 1895. Note the telegraph poles, hansom cab and premises of the Edison-Bell Phonograph Corporation. The street was formerly Cow Loan, a muddy lane leading to the pastures of Cowcaddens.

Junction of High Street and George Street looking north, c. 1900. This was the 'Bell o' the Brae', the steepest part of the medieval street. The gradient was reduced by the reforming Victorians. The corner site is under development by the City Improvement Trust. In 1901 curving crow-stepped tenements were erected on either side of High Street to the competition-winning design of Burnet, Boston and Carruthers. The tramway employee is busy keeping the crossing free of grit to prevent derailments.

High Street at Cathedral Square looking north, 1899. The electrified horse tram or 'sparkie' is bound for the south side of the city. Glasgow's first purpose-built electric trams, single-decker 'room-and-kitchen' cars, ran from Springburn to Mitchell Street. The tramway system was fully electrified in time for the 1901 International Exhibition.

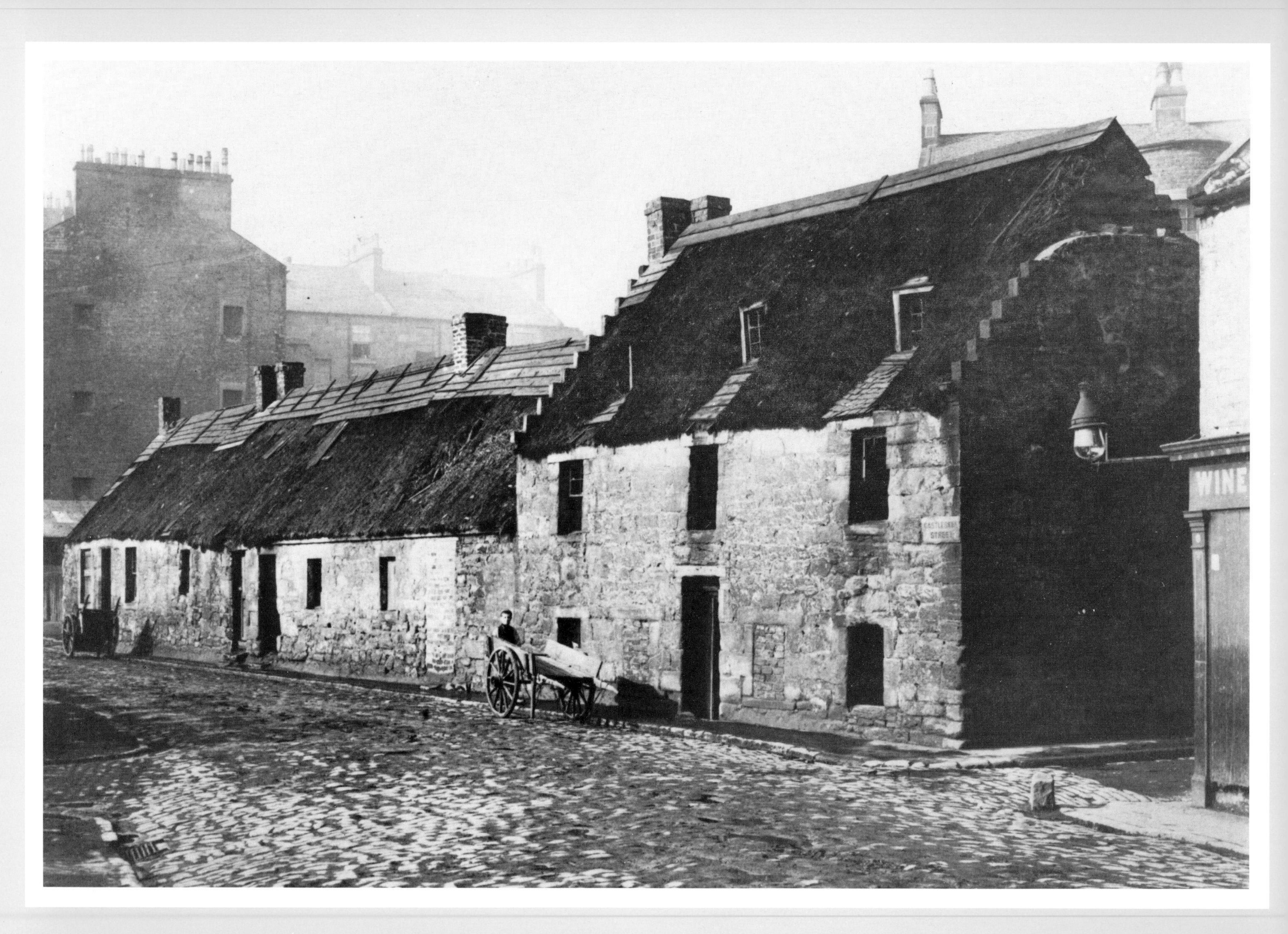

Castlebank Street, Partick, c. 1900. The street took its name from Partick Castle, built in 1611 by George Hutcheson on the right bank of the Kelvin.

Children in Hawthorn Street, Springburn, c. 1905. As early as 1885, James Burn Russell, Glasgow's second Medical Officer of Health, argued that city children deprived of opportunities for play and exercise would grow up to be poor physical specimens. His views were vindicated during the First World War, when Glasgow and other industrial cities were forced to recruit 'Bantam' battalions of much smaller-than-average men.

Sauchiehall Street looking east to Cambridge Street, c. 1905. Pettigrew and Stephen's Manchester House can be seen on the right. A chain store now occupies the site of the Balmoral Hotel. The premises of the Public House Trust exemplified the 'reformed' pubs in vogue in the early 1900s. They were financed by public-spirited citizens. The Trust had another pub in London Road.

Close at 163 Cowcaddens, c. 1910. Note the early-pattern open-flame gas lamp and the pulleys, used in lieu of drying greens. In the Edwardian period, Calton and Cowcaddens had the worst infantile mortality rates in the city.

Calton Entry, c. 1910. This was the west boundary line of the old burgh. The fish vendor in tartan shawl is perhaps trading in Loch Fyne kippers.

Steps in Wood Street, Port Dundas, 1910. With the opening of the Forth and Clyde Canal in 1790, the northern outskirts of Glasgow became a hive of industry. The children's ill-assorted clothing suggests a deplorable level of social deprivation.

Back court at Dobbie's Loan, 1910. Note the scavenger with his carrying creel. In the 17th century, Dobbie's Loan formed the access to the common pastures north-west of the town. In the mid 18th century, it became a through-road from Castle Street to Garscube Road.

Green Street, Calton, c. 1910. Camp was the trademark of a popular brand of coffee and chicory essence, produced in nearby Charlotte Street.

Buchanan Street at St. Vincent Place looking north-west towards the Western Club, Stock Exchange and St. George's Church, 1912. One of James Craig's handsome tea-rooms can be seen on the extreme right of the photograph. Before the Great War, Glasgow was said to be 'a very Tokyo for tea-rooms', the facilities of which included mahogany-panelled smoking-rooms for city merchants.

Boarding a tram in Dumbarton Road, near Hayburn Street, Partick. The photograph was taken in 1912, the year in which the burgh, with a population of 66,000, was annexed to Glasgow. At this period, the 'Standard' tram was open front and rear, and the minimum fare was a halfpenny. Horse-drawn omnibuses first ran from Glasgow to Partick Cross in the 1840s. The distinctive frontage of *The Hayburn Vaults* (1904), seen in the background, survives in pristine condition.

Stockwell Street looking south from Glassford Street, April 1914. Messrs. Mann Byars, a famous store of the period, can be seen on the extreme right. This photograph is one of a series taken during the rush hour to highlight problems of traffic congestion.

Glasgow Cross looking south-east down Saltmarket, 1916. Note the advertisement for 'New Munitions Ale'. The pub survives, renamed *The Tolbooth Bar*. The tenement on the right was designed by City Architect John Carrick in the 1880s as part of the City Improvement Trust's urban renewal programme.

Eglinton Toll looking north-east, 1917. The tenement is typical of the fine buildings erected at Glasgow street intersections, in this instance St. Andrew's Cross. On the right can be seen St. Andrew's electricity generating station, built 1899-1900, and the head office of Scott and Rae. This long-established firm of masons and builders' merchants still has offices on the same site.

Parkhead Cross looking north-west, 1923. The Clydesdale Bank now occupies the corner premises, once George Honeyman Farmer's *Vaults,* the best-known pub in the Parkhead district. For over a century the major employer in the district was Parkhead Forge founded in 1837. It closed in 1983. At the turn of the century the nuclei of Glasgow were its crosses, where several streets intersected and ornate corner tenements, befitting their position, described themselves as 'mansions'. Parkhead Cross escaped redevelopment and is now the finest of Glasgow's remaining crosses.

Argyle Street at Union Street looking north-east, 1924. By the 1930s the Argyle Hotel had been demolished and this junction had become famous as 'Boot's Corner'.

Manresa Place, Garscube Road, 1925. Note the barefoot boy with metal gird or hoop and the newspaper poster referring to 'baby farming'—unsavoury financial transactions involving unwanted children.

Corner of Norfolk Street and Warwick Street, Laurieston, c. 1928. Cumberland, Norfolk, Oxford, Portland, Salisbury and Warwick Streets testified to developers' John and David Laurie's penchant for the English nobility. The large brick building was a bonded warehouse owned by the Glasgow Bonding Company.

Junction of Renfield Street and Bath Street looking east, 1930. Stylish Art Deco restaurants such as Ross's Corner House were a feature of the new Glasgow street architecture of the 1930s.

Argyle Street at Union Street looking north-east, 1930. The celebrated 'Boot's Corner', trysting-place of generations of Glaswegians. From the 1960s onwards, the stone neo-Georgian facade of the Adelphi Hotel was hidden behind a blue and yellow curtain wall. At the time of writing, the site is undergoing redevelopment.

Charing Cross looking west, 1930. The Grand Hotel (1878), the dominant feature of Glasgow's gateway to the West End, would not have looked out of place in the Paris of Napoleon III. It was demolished in 1968 to make way for the M8 motorway.

Prince's Restaurant, 96 St. Vincent Street, 1931. Page boys in Grand Hotel-style uniforms were also seen in large numbers in the cinemas of the 1930s. St. Vincent Street, one of the finest thoroughfares in Glasgow's second New Town, was opened in 1804. By mid-century, its terraced houses were already being adapted for commercial use, and purpose-built office blocks such as the famous 'Hatrack'—a Victorian skyscraper on a single house plot—followed in due course.

Greenhaugh Street, Govan, 1932. The canopied entrance led to Govan Subway Station. From 1896 to 1935 the trains were powered by cable haulage.

Rogart Street, Bridgeton, 1933. Backlands such as this were typical of the cramped and insanitary conditions prevailing in working class districts.

The Rabbie Burns (153 Trongate), still flourishing when this photograph was taken in 1938, was a popular late Victorian hostelry. With its collection of Burnsiana, it rivalled neighbouring attractions such as the Britannia music hall and Macleod's Waxworks.

Union Street, 1938. *The Union Café* at number 116 was opened in 1901 by the restaurateur William Hunter. It was owned at this period by John Y. Whyte, proprietor of the famous *Horseshoe Bar* in Drury Street. The *Café* has since vanished, but its stained glass Union Jack pendants are preserved in the *Horseshoe Bar*. Note the references to those 1930s obsessions, beauty culture and permanent waves.

Slum property near the corner of Commerce Street and Nelson Street, Tradeston, 1946. The brick toilets would have been added as a result of a local act of parliament in 1890.

Lawmoor Street, Hutchesontown, 1947. Despite the poignant graffiti these were hardly homes fit for heroes. In 1951 almost 42 per cent of the population of Gorbals were living more than two to a room. Less than half the houses had an inside lavatory and fewer than one in ten had a bath.

Hope Street looking north from Argyle Street, c. 1950. From 1906 onwards, this section of the street was dominated by the huge train hall of Central Station and the adjoining Station Hotel, built on the site of the old village of Grahamston. Note the milk bar on the right hand side of the street.

Glassford Street looking south from Ingram Street with the Trades House on the right, 1954. Trolleybuses had a brief heyday from their introduction in April 1949 to May 1967 when they were finally withdrawn from service.

Cumberland Street, Hutchesontown, looking north-west, 1955. Matheson Lane is on the extreme right. The photographer was standing opposite the Paragon Cinema, a former United Free Church.

The Queen Arcade, 1960. Named in honour of Queen Victoria, it ran from Renfrew Street to Cowcaddens. 'J. H. Muir', writing in 1901, described it as 'a place of trumpets (in brass), foreign stamps, scraps, transfers, drawing slates, socialistic pamphlets, and old books.'

Moffat Street, Hutchesontown, 1955, looking south towards the Southern Necropolis, with Govan Iron Works—'Dixon's Blazes'—in the distance. The corner pub was named after the licensee rather than the fictional detective.

North Street, Anderston, 1958. The eighteenth century village of Anderston grew into a manufacturing town during the 19th century and the weavers' thatched cottages gave way to tenements, which in turn were demolished in the Comprehensive Development of the district during the 1970s. North Street, known in the early days of the village as 'the Lang Road', was originally a narrow tree-lined path. The surviving portion of the street now runs parallel to the M8 motorway.

St. Enoch's Square looking north, c. 1960. The huge steel and glass St. Enoch Centre now occupies the site of the Station Hotel (1875-9), demolished in 1977. In the 1780s St. Enoch's Square (1782) and George Square (1786) marked the western extremity of Glasgow.

Tower block under construction in Hutchesontown-Gorbals Comprehensive Development Area, c. 1965.